Mountain

Acorns

and

Butterflies

Melanie —
My wish is that something
in here touches your heart.
[signature]

Written By

Pete McKechnie

Design and Layout by

Nancy Smaroff

ISBN-9781793294708

Previous books:

Mountain Top Musing (Vol I)
*A Reluctant Poet's Glimpse
Into His Own Heart*

Mountain Top Musing (Vol II)
*Along the Path of
The Warrior Poet's Heart
Tenderness Awaits*

Mountain Top Musing (Vol III)
Reflections

Watch:

"Pete McKechnie" on YouTube

Follow:

Pete's work on Facebook at
"Mountain Top Muse"

Contact info:

mountaintopmuse@gmail.com

"Like the roots of a tree, I reach
Deep into my mother,
Connected, intertwined.
And with each breath, I understand
That her breath
Is taken as mine."

~ Pete McKechnie

In those moments when I am silent and open…

As a theme, the natural world runs deep in this collection. It is true, however, that all of the poems and none of them are ultimately about the natural world. It is also true that all of poems, and none of them, were inspired by the natural world. What is most true is that being in nature and spending time alone outside does something to me, creates something like a silence within me. And then, on those blissful evenings I find myself composing, a truly mundane thing will happen, and the words just flow. There are a few in this collection that to me speak most clearly to this. 'Copperhead' and 'The Crows' were real-life experiences I had over 20 years ago, one before I had started even writing poetry. Neither came to be until recently, and when they came to be, neither was on my mind. Something simply happened while I was in a moment of silence, sparked a memory, and decades later both stories landed on paper. Another, 'The Feather,' is similar in many ways, other than the time differential. This one was almost immediate. A short walk on my property gifted me with footprints of a Great Blue heron. Not long after that, 100 or so feet, a feather. I did not think to write, though I held the feather for a few moments before placing it back on the ground. Hours later, in the silent aftermath of my day, a friend posted on social media about the excitement that can come on a walk through the woods and a feather is spotted on the forest floor.

Less than 5 minutes later, 'The Feather' was born. It wasn't the feather that inspired it, and it wasn't a post about a feather that inspired it. It was the thread between the two, and silence, that brought them together and turned them into words. This is how it happens for me; silence, a space I recognize when I am graced with it, and the most random and mundane of inspirations. I don't create the web that creates the poem, I just follow it in those moments I am silent and open enough to recognize it.

Within this sunrise

My heart pauses,

And understands;

There is no beauty more precious

Than this moment,

And as the sun rises higher,

My heart soars and knows,

That nothing will prevent

The ascension of my soul.

~Pete McKechnie

Contents

The Feather

I see it on the path.

White, tipped with black,

And instantly I hear its call

Though around me

The forest is silent.

I pick it up,

Feeling it, stroking it,

Until the vanes meet,

Forming a perfect feather.

The sensation is sublime,

The beauty immense,

And I place it gently on the ground,

Thanking nature for a mental image

Of a bird I cannot see.

Dawn's Gift

Dawn's light shines,
Once again,
On my shoulders.

This morning, however,
The sensation culminates.
The sensation,
Though familiar to
Many other sunrises
And familiar
To my senses,
Finally speaks to my heart.

Finally, sunrise gives me
The understanding
That not only will
All nights end,
They will all end
In the awakening
That is sought.

With this new understanding,
I welcome this dawn,
And find within myself
The strength
To help others see,
It is only after the
Darkest of nights
That the power of dawn's gift
Can be fully
Embraced by the soul.

Passage

As the sun rises each morning,
It rises over a changed landscape.
These changes, though countless,
Are often indiscernible.
The landscape, each morning,
Looks basically the same.

It is only with time
That we understand
And discern
The subtle shifts.

It is only with time
That we come to witness
Our own growth,
And understand
That, while each day
We might wake up
Basically the same,
It is with the passage of time
That we will come
To see our truth.

Silence

I have sat alone in the woods,
Listening to a silence
That was deafening to my ears.

I have witnessed occurrences
That meant the world to me
Even as they passed
Without sound.

And what has this meant to me?

The world speaks
Most profoundly
Without words.
It is in silence
We most often find the meaning
That points our hearts
In the direction
Our souls are meant to travel.

What More Could You Ask?

What more could you ask of me?

I would kill for you.
I would die for you.
I would shadow you through your darkest times.
I would ask nothing in return
As I bartered my very soul
That your heart might beat once more.

What more could you ask of me?

You could pour out your heart to me,
Tell me secrets destined for no other ears,
And though I look at you with quizzical eyes,
Head cocked to betray my confusion,
You will feel the compassion in my soul.

What more could I ask of you?

That you keep me fed,
Be in the moment, as I always am,
When you play my games with me.
And that I am allowed to be what I am,
A soul born of wolves, bred by man,
Wild at heart, tame by decree, loyal by nature.

What more could you ask of me?
I am your dog.

The Dreamer's Dream

Is it the bird
Who builds a nest,
Or the nest
That builds a bird?
One begets the other
And without both
The egg withers,
Dies.

It is the same
With dreams and dreamers.
The dreamer
Builds the nest
In which the dream
Can manifest,
Allowing the dream
To awaken
And the dreamer
To come alive.

Cycle of Becoming

It is easy to believe
At the end of a brilliant day
That the moon follows the sun.

It is easy to believe
That darkness follows light.

I wonder.
The sun brings growth,
It brings a vibrancy
And a passion
That cannot be found in darkness.

The moon
Illuminates a silence,
A pause.
The moon occupies the space
Between growth,
And gives birth to understanding.

Perhaps it is not true
That the moon follows the sun,
Any more than darkness follows light.

Perhaps it is truth
That they dance together
In an endless cycle
Of becoming.

The Acorn

Don't let me go, the acorn pleads
As it clings to its branch.

But I must.

Why? I will fall to the forest floor,
I will become fodder for all,
Or rot into the ground.

Yes... or...?

Or what?

Or you will sprout, and become,
And someday have this talk
With your own acorns.

But what if I do not sprout?
What if I just fall?

Then your fate
Would be the same as it would be
If I never let you go.

Release

As the autumn winds blow,

Do the trees dread the shedding of their leaves?

Do they fear the naked branches,

Exposed to the winds?

Or

Do they perceive the potential for growth,

After the dark season passes,

And give themselves willingly

To the season's transformation?

Butterfly

You have touched me,
More deeply,
And with more truth,
Than I can express.

You have reached
Into places
Hidden for eons
From the light,
And allowed
My deepest recesses
To shine.

You have held me,
More closely,
And with more truth,
Than I can express.

You have guided me
To places
I would never
Have dared to explore,
And allowed
My deepest desires
To express.

You have loved me
Unabashedly,
And with more passion
Than I can understand,
Deeper and truer
Than any other.

Now, you have
Set me free,
To Love.

For this,
My darling,
I thank you.

Perennial Faith

Autumn approaches
And with faith
The perennial flora bows.
With faith
They give in,
Give up life,
Knowing
That winter
Will not last forever.

With spring,
Enough of them
Will awaken,
Enough of their essence
Will survive
To ensure
That come next year's
Darker days
Their numbers will
Ensure another cycle's
Awakening…

Season's Gifts

Each winter fades to spring, giving up the
Silent, brilliant wonderland of
White to a
Burst of growth.

And each spring fades to summer, giving up the
Explosive, brilliant wonderland of
Birth to the
Maturity of growth.

Each summer fades to autumn, giving up the
True, brilliant wonderland of
Fullness to the
Waning light.

And each autumn fades to winter, allowing the
Silent, brilliant wonderland of
Life to be
Re-born.

Thrive

The underbrush does not look
To the treetops
And wonder,

What could I be if I could be that?

And the trees
Do not look down
And wonder,

Why can't you grow?

The underbrush simply
Provides the forage,
The canopy the shade,
And together life thrives.

So, I will not ask you
What you might want of me,
And I will not seek
To give you what you desire.
I will simply express
And hope that you
Simply express as well.

A Single Seed

It is as if failure
Is the nature of life.
One needs only
To take a walk,
To witness a forest floor
Scattered with thousands of acorns
Which lay rotting on the ground,
To understand this.

It is as if failure
Is the nature of life.
It might seem obvious, in reality,
That there is no point.
Why try,
When so much of our effort
Will lie useless on the ground?
This denies a simple truth,
And fails to understand
The true nature of life.

While a multitude
Of the seeds we sow
Will fall silently to the ground,
It is the single seed
That only perseverance can sow
Which will grow
Into the true nature of our legacy.

Winter's Gift

I feel winter's grip loosening.
I feel her frigid fingers letting go.
   I find myself thankful.

Thankful for the promise
Of the coming spring,
But, thankful, also,
For the solitude
And introspection offered
   By the depths of winter's darkness.

It is not so much
That the darkness of winter
Holds me down, restrains me.
It is more that winter's embrace
   Cradles me, holds me silent.

As one growing season ebbs
And is reborn in another,
   I revel in this time of darkness.

I thrive through the freeze,
Because I know that this is just
   Another part of the cycle of my growth.

Transitions

Silence abides

As the skies darken,

As the stars,

One by one,

Illuminate.

This silence brings peace.

This silence allows

Me to sit,

To witness,

The beauty of the light

As it gives way

To the beauty of the darkness.

As the light fades,

The darkness exposes

In its own beauty

The truth that dawn will

Follow shortly

With a new day.

Illumination

I WAIT.
In the fading light
The moon's white glow
Replaces the fading gold
Of the sun.

I KNOW.
The sun's light
Gives way to the moon,
And it is the
White light of the moon
Which most effectively
Illuminates my life.

The Witness

"Do you see me?" I ask.
"Do you hear me?" I ask Creation, I ask God.

It is a lament.

Then sunrise comes
And I witness
The world awakening
Before me.
I hear the songs
Of Creation
Resonating around me
And I realize,
That for me
To be experiencing
These awakenings,
They must also
Be experiencing me.

So my question,
"Am I heard, seen by God, Creation?"
Is meaningless.

In order for me to witness Creation,
God and Creation must be witnessing me.

Act of Creation

Is it the leaf or the tree
Which lets go
As nights grow longer
And the days grow colder?

Is it the leaf which knows
Its destiny is to fall to the forest floor?
Or is it the tree which knows
That Spring's incipient bud
Will not manifest
Lest last year's growth be shed?

Perhaps it is both.
Perhaps letting go
Is more a mutual act of creation
Than an individual act of will.

Fullness

As I watch the moon tonight,
High in the sky,
Half full, waxing,
I realize it would
Be no less beautiful
If I did not know
That it is growing for now,
And not fading nightly 'til new.

This can be said for life.
I don't know
Which moments
Signify the unfolding to fullness,
Or which moments
Are the advance of darkness.
Yet, when I witness
Them in singularity,
In the moment,
They are all beautiful
In their own right.
They are all part of the cycle
Of darkness and light,
Neither of which
Can reach fullness
Without the other.

Symphony

As the wind whistles

Through the forest,

Each trunk and branch

Plays a different note

In the symphony of the storm.

Playing My Part

I stood tonight, outside,
Just for a few moments,
And gazed into the sky.
As I peered into the mystery
That is our night sky,
I pondered briefly
Just how far away
Those dots of light are,
And how disconnected I can feel
At times from my universe.

I began to hear
The nightly symphony.
I began to pay attention
To the myriad of creatures
Who call out each night,
In an attempt to simply sing their song.

An understanding unfolds…

I do not need to comprehend
The mysteries of the universe
In order to play my role in it,
Any more that the crickets
And frogs in my yard
Need to understand theirs.
I simply need to play it,
And sing my song,
And that it is the simple act
Of playing a role,
And singing a song,
Which will ensure my connection to all.

Smaller

Could I feel smaller
Than when standing outside at night,
Witnessing the magical nature
Of the night sky?

Could I not get
That the magnitude
Of what is before me
Dwarfs me,
Swallows me,
And makes me meaningless
In the grand scheme of things?

How could I not understand that?
How could I not know
That the simple act
Of witnessing the universe
Makes my presence in it irrelevant?

I hear in the background
Of my meaningless life
The songs of nature,
The songs that make my world beautiful.
I understand immediately
That the beauty
Of the expansive night sky
Is defined by the mundane lives
Being experienced there,
Just as my mundane life here
And the songs of my world's creatures,
Make this little dot of light
Inspirational to those
Who might witness it
From millions of light years away.

Into the Thorns

I could choose to sit on this bench,
'Neath the clear blue sky
And witness the park around me
From the safety of my perch.

I could choose to wander
A manicured path,
Which both brings me closer
To the reality around me
But still allows me to step aside.

I could choose to step off this path,
Mingle among the trees,
And witness the world around me
From the relative safety of the forest.

I could choose to delve deeper,
Into the wilderness,
Which will bring me closer
To the reality around me,
Making the choice to step aside
More difficult.

I could choose to risk the brambles
And give myself the understanding,
That a life without thorns
Will never allow me
To live among the roses.

Transformation

As the butterfly

Cannot speed the transition

From chrysalis to wings,

But merely be present

To the transformation,

I cannot force an awakening.

I can merely be here,

Where I am,

And allow it to unfold.

This is a simple truth

Of the transformative life.

While the butterfly

Might be destined to grow wings,

It must first

Embrace the chrysalis,

And I must first fully

Embrace each stage I find myself in

If I am to be able to

Embrace my truth.

The Wilderness

I walk into this wilderness, blind,
Following a call I truly can't discern.
It is unclear what might lie within this wilderness,
Yet the draw is undeniable,
An irresistible force guiding me forth.

Into this wilderness I will walk, blind,
Following a truth that escapes me.
With time, it becomes clear,
That what lies within this wilderness
Is the draw of my soul,
The irresistible force bringing me home.

Give me this time in the wilderness,
And allow me to delve into its mystery.
This is the gift, the compass,
That will bring me to myself.

Rebirth

As I celebrate this day,
And welcome the birth of Spring,
My partner, somewhere to the south,
Laments the shortening days,
His summer ending in autumn's birth.
Soon, for me,
The growing light will end,
At the solstice,
And my days, too, will dwindle.

This day should be
The reminder of balance,
As soon the greatest
Light of the north
Will be met
With the greatest
Darkness of the south,
And the cycle will begin anew.

This dance of light and dark,
This waxing and waning,
Shows us that without both,
There is no chance of rebirth.

The Vessel

In the same way
That a seed does not ask
Into what it should grow,
It merely falls to the forest floor and sprouts,
A spirit does not ask
What it is meant to express,
It simply enters a body and is born.

However, in the same way
That the virility of the soil
Dictates the seed's ability to grow,
It is the silent agendas
And perceptions of the mind
That can cloud the spirit's expression.

It is not the farmer's job
To dictate the growth of the seed,
but merely to prepare the soil.
It is not our job
To dictate the path of our soul,
It is merely to understand
That we are simply the vessel
For its expression.

Reflection

In search of myself, I speak to Creation.
Asking for a hint, a clue, of what I am to become.

Who am I? I ask.
What do you want from me?
How do I find my path?

Through the stillness a pull, a tug,
And I set off through the woods.

Guided, in every step,
Ever deeper into the forest,
Ever deeper into myself,
I can feel the anticipation of
My answer building.

I arrive, eventually, along the banks of a small creek,
And as I kneel to slake my thirst,
I see my reflection in the water,
And I understand.

Should I Simply...

Should I try? Really?

Should I strive, endeavor to create myself

As I would love to be?

Or should I instead be like the acorn,

Which falls and lands,

Is devoured or covered,

And sometimes, without effort or struggle,

Grows into the mighty oak?

Should I try? Really?

Should I try to take control of this life

And create myself?

Or should I allow the landing guided by fate

The opportunity to create what simply 'is?'

Should I try?

Or should I simply be?

The Snowflake

The snowflake falls, inconsequential.
A mere speck of white
On the dark ground of Winter.

A snowflake is powerless on its own,
The bitter ground of Winter
Swallowing it, uncaring.

Yet when the snowflakes fly,
When they come together,
And cover the dark grounds of Winter
In a blanket of white,
They will melt away into the dark soil
And bring with it the beauty of Spring.

The Coming Year

Another year almost over,
Another cycle near complete,
Release once more an option.

Let me enter
The bitter winds of winter
By undressing, disrobing,
Removing the garments
I have so clearly outgrown,
And those which have clearly
Outgrown me.

Let me end this cycle naked,
With dreams and hopes
As well as fears and failures
Folded neatly on the floor
Next to me,
Allowing me to let go and embrace
This next cycle exposed,
And ready to become.

The Blossom

Why so sad, Blossom?

Well, the bees
Have not come
To visit today.

*Didn't I see
A hummingbird grace
Your petals earlier?*

Well yes,
But she is gone,
And I am left alone.

*A butterfly after that,
I saw it land gently
And drink deeply.*

Ah, yes.
But she too is gone,
And I am alone.

*So you have missed
The gift of the hummingbird
And butterfly,
While waiting for the bee?*

Well, no... I mean,
Where are the bees?

Talk to me tomorrow, Blossom,
While the bees
Drink your essence,
And the hummingbirds
Fly elsewhere.
Because tomorrow
You will lament
That the hummingbirds
Have not come to visit.

What would you have me do?

Well, Blossom,
I would have you open
To whatever gift is offered,
And not worry yourself
If the gift comes as a bee,
A hummingbird
Or a butterfly.
I would have you understand
That any gift
which brings fruition
To your blossom
Is a gift that allows you to grow.

ALWAYS LOVE

A lways, the sun sets,

    L ets go

        W ithout regret or remorse

        A nd ready, willing,

            Y earning to give itself to night

                S haring itself with the darkness.

L ove, the sun knows,

    O pens in darkness and

        V irtue reborn,

            E nvelopes the night.

The Seed Presents

The seed presents, regardless.
It does not wait or hesitate.
It does not fear the possibilities.
It merely sprouts when the time is right.

The following days might bring
A freeze or a drought,
And the seed might not survive.

But it presents and sprouts,
Because that is what it must do
In order to express the
Unique beauty it holds.

The seed presents, regardless.
The seed understands that it is not
Life nor death that matters.
It is the expression of its unique truth
That counts.

Singing Our Beauty

Perhaps the first is the crocus,
Bursting forth in early Spring,
Sometimes through the snow,
And crying out,
Aren't I beautiful?

Before long, perhaps, a carpet of gold,
The dandelion asking the same.
Soon the dogwood and redbud will compete,
Each presenting its flowers to the meadow.
Each asking,
Aren't I beautiful?

The seasons draw on with the
Purple/White globes of the milkweed,
And brilliant yellows of goldenrod,
But still the quest,
The question is,
Aren't I beautiful?

As the seasons end and the meadow
Prepares itself for winter,
The meadow looks down,
And sees,
Aren't I beautiful?

But the meadow does not know,
That across the ridge to the West,
And the valley to the North,
Across the seas to the East
And the forests to the South
Lie countless other meadows.

And the Earth rests with the passage
Of the seasons, and knows,
Yes, we are beautiful.

Love in the Storm

How many of us would dance in the rain?
How many would accept the downpours,
And choose to embrace them,
Not to hide indoors and escape?

How many of us would make love
Outside in a thunderstorm,
To experience a lover's passion
In the ferocity of lightning's dance?
Not many of us, perhaps,
Because dancing in the sun is easy,
And making love in comfort is as well.

But life is not easy, nor comfortable,
And will only be understood
With the balance
Between the sunny days which bring comfort
And the stormy days which bring passion.

To dance within the raindrops
And make love, even in the storm,
Brings fullness to our lives.
So, dance in the sun and in the rain
Make love in comfort and in the storm.
Dance and make love.

The Caterpillar

Though tied together,
More tightly than night and day,
The caterpillar will never know the butterfly.
And the butterfly, upon awakening,
Will not remember its days crawling on the branches.

The caterpillar lives and
Gives birth to the butterfly,
And the butterfly lives
To give birth to the caterpillar,
But they will never meet each other,
They will never understand the depths to which
Their destinies are entwined.

This is us.
We give birth.
We take flight.
We crawl on the branches,
Then spread our wings.
But we don't, at any given moment,
See the masterpiece that our lives
Will endeavor to create.

A Better Dream?

Should I wonder?

Should I allow myself to dream?

Would I dream a better dream?

Than the sun's touch on a flower?

Than the wind's gentle whisper through the trees?

Than the eternal flow from the mountains to the seas?

Could I dream a bigger dream?

Than sunlight's kiss on a leaf?

Than a droplet of water on a petal?

No, I think I cannot dream a better dream,

And I should not even try.

Sunset

There is wisdom,
And there is joy,
In a sunset.

Many, if not most, will miss this.
Many, if not most, will lament
Spring's passing, youth's passing,
And risk missing the fruition of growth.

Many, if not most, will see sunset as an end.
Sunset, in fact, is not an end, but a culmination.

I will welcome my sunset.
I will appreciate the chance to look back,
And see how everything I have had a part in
Has grown, thrived, and matured.

And while my sun may be setting,
The Sun of my creations is riding high noon,
And the Suns they will create are waiting to arise.

On the Wind

Could I have thought this moment?

Can a single Angel from a dandelion's head think,
Over there is where I will grow next year?

Can I imagine my fate any more than a seed
As it floats in the wind, not waiting to land
As landings are not yet in their experience?

I am thinking not.
I am thinking I will never know what I will become.

I am thinking that the best I can do is to
Enjoy the currents as they carry me,
And should I land, grow happily from there,
And allow the next gust of wind
To carry me on.

Nature's Dance

The sky is darkening,
And on the winds,
The sound of distant thunder carries.

Yet, as I stand on my porch,
The sounds of frogs resonate.

The sounds of life carrying-on
In the face of the imminent storm
Fills my ears.

Yes, I think,
The storm is coming.
And, yes, I think
I will dance in this rain.

The Kingdom

The lion is not dishonest
As it stalks the gazelle.
They both know the scoop,
And both try to ensure
Their own agenda.

This is true
With predator and prey
Throughout the Kingdom,
With but one exception, Us.

We no longer kill to survive,
We kill to thrive,
And with that
We have brought a level
Of deceit, dishonesty,
Not known, in the least,
To the Kingdom
Into which we were born.

Stirring My Soul

Why does a sunset fill me?
Why does witnessing
The brilliant colors
Fading beneath the mountains
Stir my soul?

I don't know
Any more than I know
Why sunrise fills me,
Or why it is
That dawn's awakening
Speaks so clearly
To my soul.

I do know
I love these things.
For now, and forever,
That is all I need to know.

Copperhead

Her copper scales glistened in the sun.
A thin patchwork of black nylon garden net
Constricting her, killing her,
Trapping her in a march to certain death.

This is how I found her,
Copper hour-glass embroiled in black lace.
Amber eyes and diamond head
Watching me, warning me.
I thought to dispatch her,
To ease her suffering,
Until I looked at my son.

The choice before me,
Free her from suffering and risk nothing,
Or free her and risk a bite.
I turned to my son and said
We have to help her...

With a tiny pair of scissors, I went to work.

My hand inches from her mouth.

She would flinch as I worked the pointed scissors

Under the thin nylon strands,

Clipping one, then the next, then the next…

As if there was an understanding,

She never bit, or even opened her mouth,

And one by one the choking strands were cut.

She was free at last.

We watched her slither away through the yard,

Her brilliant copper scales glistening.

For me, how much more

Incredible it was to have saved her,

Than merely to have

Saved her from her suffering.

Destiny of the Flower

The flower reaches out toward the sun.
This is fate — necessary, and dangerous.

Fruition is the path, exposure the key.
The key opens,
Not only the door to fruition,
But to consumption.

So, the flower will reach to the sun, it must.
And though it may be eaten,
Its fate if it did not reach out, open,
Would be the same as if it were
Plucked from the Earth by a deer.

In this reaching out, there is risk.
And while it may be sealed,
Its fate cannot be lived without it.

The Heron and I

The heron stalks my pond as do I.
But the heron stalks quietly, unseen,
As I stalk clumsily, noticed.

We both, however, feed our needs.

The heron stalks,
And with luck feeds, filling its belly.
Me, I stalk filling my senses.
Both, with a walk around my pond,
Will find ourselves fulfilled.

So walk around my pond, Heron,
And fill your belly.
I will walk around it
And fill my soul.

Tiny Forces, Guiding

The urban sidewalk was not mine.
I felt trapped, out of step
In my attempt just to breathe,
Just to be outside.

From my self-induced prison,
Standing alone along
City streets that were not my own,
I opened, and allowed myself to see.

Walking past me was a dog — a small dog.
And dragged behind this little being
Was a full-grown adult, leash in hand.
But it was most certainly the little dog
Who was in charge of the walk.

I watched this walk.
At first with humour, then judgment,
I watched as this little dog
Dragged its owner here and there.

Then I saw, and understood.
I was not trapped in this distant city
Along this sidewalk.
I was trapping myself.
And just like the little dog
Was dragging his master along,
I allowed the tiny things
To have power over me
And drag me wherever they chose.

As the little dog and its master left my sight,
I understood.
I will never be powerless,
I will never be left to the whims of others,
Unless, I willingly succumb to a will
That is not my own.

Longest Night

Once again, the sun sets
Ushering in the longest night.
Ushering in the greatest
Darkness there will be.

And once again, the sun will rise
At the dawn of this
Longest night,
And light
Will be brought back
To this world.

Blessed Solstice

Moments of Grace

I walk through the pasture,
Much of the time
My eyes fixed on the horizon.
Much of the time
My feet senselessly moving forward
As my attention is
Elsewhere, in the distance.

Moments of grace shift this.
Moments of grace alter my perspective.

And allow me to walk through the pasture,
My eyes taking in all that is around me.

And I find myself Thankful.

Thankful that I choose
To witness the moment
And not the horizon.

All Lives

The buck is in my sights.
I can see him breathing,
His nostrils sensing the air.
Free, living, and I can end it all
With the pull of a trigger.
I can feed my life by ending his.

I don't.
The trigger I pull is a camera,
And I capture his image in a photo.

And later, as I eat a tender steak,
Grown and killed on a feedlot,
I feel good about myself
Because I can gaze at a picture
Of an animal I did not kill,
And believe that my meal did not result
In the death of one of God's creatures.

Sustenance is in my sights.

It breathes, it lives on the air,

Free and living.

And I, at the end of it all,

Need to understand,

That I will not have life

Unless I am responsible for the death

Of another of God's creations.

My choice is to

Honour the lives that feed me, or not.

My choice is to

Honour life, or not.

By Any Other Name

What is a flower?
A delicate strand of manifest sunlight,
A subtle fragrance
Drifting seductively with the breeze,
Petals soft as lips
Kissing the hummingbird's cheeks.
The womb of seeds, nourishing generations.

What is a flower?
Inspiration for poets, magic for lovers,
Lying scattered or clustered
In blankest of vibrant color,
Pure and timeless greetings
Of love and remorse.
Cut or cultivated,
They touch the heart, and caress the soul.

What is a flower?
It is life,
It is love.

Moment-by-Moment

Crows call out their welcome
To the rising sun,
Flying erratically
On the gusty breeze.

Woodpeckers calling out,
Peck-peck-pecking on trees
Sending a resonant thunder
That echoes through the forest.

Clouds drifting gently,
Spitting snow as they pass.
Quietly shading, then exposing
The ever-present sun.

Fruition and Sustenance

The Monarch simply feeds.
It does not know
That a milkweed plant
Is its sustenance, its destiny.
It simply feeds.

And the milkweed
Wanting nothing more
Than to sow its seed,
Doesn't know
That the Monarch
Is its truth.

But they grow,
And depend on each other,
As one flies south,
And the other spreads its seeds
To the wind.

From My Dog

Hmm, Sky Raisins,
I will hunt you down.
Devour your tender
Deliciousness.

I will break my leash
In my attempt
To catch you little
Winged morsels.
I will smash into
The countertops, bookshelves,
Pounce back and forth
In a path of destruction
As you fly around
In a desperate attempt
To escape me.

My human seems
To dislike this.
It tries to dissuade me.
But, hmm, Sky Raisins,
I will catch you,
And enjoy your tender
Deliciousness.

Vanishing

So many years ago that I cannot count.
A life time, really, perhaps several.

In that life, as a child,
Each summer night
Was greeted with the dance
Of the firefly on the breeze.
Hundreds, it seemed,
Too many to catch, shining proud
In a small patch of urban America.

Years, and lifetimes, pass.
And now, even in my rural setting,
The dance of the firefly is obscure.
Even here, well beyond the city's light,
The dance is curtailed.

I don't have to wonder why.
I know that the firefly lives in the grass,
And I know that we poison the grass
To ensure a perfect lawn.
I know that our desire to curtail the weeds
Is also limiting our opportunity to witness
The beautiful dance of the firefly
On a summer's eve.

So many years ago that I cannot count.
A lifetime, really.

Tooth of the Lion

Brilliant globe of yellow,
Toothed leaves
With roots digging
Deep into the Earth.

We lament these,
We dis-honour their beauty,
In our attempt to create
A lawn of uniformity.

We will not win this battle.
The 'Tooth of the Lion' will win.
Our lawns will always bloom
With brilliant yellow globes,
And I am thankful,
Because I know,
That the Dandelion will thrive.

Lamb's Quarters

Each year planted by the wind,
And each year,
Tilled, hoed, pulled.

Each year I present myself,
Amid the farmer's planted seeds,
And watch as corn, beans,
Squash are planted,
Even as I am
Pulled from the ground, discarded.

But each year, I come back,
My arrow leaves offering,
Opening myself to a harvest
Far greater than compost.

Each year, I give myself
To the farmer, whose vision
Will someday see me.

Each year, I come back,
Carried by the wind. discarded,
Yet offering myself
To a hidden harvest
Amongst the coveted plants.

And someday the farmer
Will see me for what I am,
A weed, for sure,
But one that grows
Without effort,
And offers sustenance.

Each year, I come back.
Take me, use me, see me.
Honour the gift
I offer, as a simple weed.

Purpose

Connection happens,
Without agenda.

It happens
As the hummingbird
Hovers
Over a flower,
And sips its
Sweet nectar.

It happens
As the honey bee
Drinks the essence
From the purple thistle.

It happens,
If we allow it,
In each moment
We live.

Let me
Live the moment
That the hummingbird
Drinks,
And the honey bee
Thrives,
Because this
Is the point,
And the purpose of my life.

My Dog

My dog barks, and I thank her.

I see nothing outside.

Well, maybe a sparrow.

Maybe nothing, except

The wind is dancing with the trees.

But I thank her, for barking.

My dog barks, and I thank her.

She is keeping me safe,

From the sparrow,

Or from nothing,

But it doesn't matter,

She barks, and keeps me safe.

It doesn't matter,

Because I keep the door closed

And we are safe.

My dog barks, and I thank her.

And think, what the hell,

Let's just go outside.

The sparrows fly,

And the wind dances with the leaves.

I realize, her bark

Was never meant to keep me safe,

It was meant to welcome me

To everything that I was missing

Beyond my door.

My dog barks, and I tell her,

Good girl, Thank you.

My Garden

I walk my garden, pulling one plant

So another can thrive.

I weed, so one plant will live, and another die.

This is a choice I make.

This directs the fruition of my garden.

Sometimes, it is necessary.

Sometimes,

Pulling a thistle from my garden,

And denying a butterfly its future meal

Is what gives me mine.

Sometimes, a weed pulled equals a fruit harvested.

Sometimes,

I witness a butterfly sipping nectar

From a thistle not growing in my garden.

It is these moments that open my eyes.

I can tend my garden,

Weed to my heart's content,

And with this effort

Control my fenced in patch of fruit.

Or I can absorb the beauty

Of my yard's weeds,

And allow them to feed not only me, but all.

So, I will tend my garden.

I will pull a weed.

I will allow the golden squash to bloom.

But I will also allow

The brilliant purple thistle to grow in my yard,

And feed the butterfly

Like my tiny patch of garden feeds me.

The Crows

Serpentine road, leading me home.

Ahead, a black pile of feathers,

A dead crow,

Killed earlier by some car

In front of me.

I stopped,

Picked up the crow.

My intention to take a few feathers,

Place it off the road,

And offer some thanks for its life.

Feathers taken when I got home,

Body left outside,

And in no time at all,

A chorus of crows began singing,

Screaming,

Circling over their dead comrade,

Knowing that the body in my yard

Was their own.

I went back out,

And gathered up the dead crow,

Walking it farther from the house,

Dropping to my knees.

Angry crows were circling

As I thanked this lovely creature

For its life and its gift,

Aho, I thought,

Let your spirit fly free now.

And the angry crows dispersed.

All they wanted,

It was clear to me,

Was that I honour the life

From which I had taken this gift.

Nightly Chorus

The night's chorus resonates
With places so deeply within me
That it can't be measured.
Stepping outside, hearing the song that
Became part of my soul years ago…
And I am there,
On a porch as a child,
Glass doors wide open,
Listening to my favourite song.

A time of innocence,
A time when my greatest concern
Was no more than mist
On my windshield
Might be now.

On a porch, the call of Nature
Pulling me to dream.
A song that tells me
All is right in this world,
And in the morning
I will awaken, refreshed.
The night's chorus resonates.
And I hear on the breath of the wind,
All that can be right
In this world.

Peckerwood

Distant thunder in the woods,
Reverberating
Resonating
As an announcement of presence,
An expression of a search.

Simplistically
A search for a mate,
But no it is deeper.
It is a search
For the one who hears
The deep drumming
And recognizes a soulmate.

Along with the resonating drum
What appears to be only a hole
In a tree takes shape.
A simple hole,
Unless
Time is spent in awe,
Witnessing over time
As one by one
Fledglings appear.
And, one by one,
Take flight
In search of the perfect tree
On which to broadcast their truth.

Sometimes I wonder –

Is it the roots
That support the tree?

Or the tree
Which supports the roots?

For when the mighty oak falls,
It is the very flesh of the Mother
Which tears.

34131827R00049

Made in the USA
Middletown, DE
24 January 2019